Celtic Nature Prayers

Prayers from an Ancient Well

Celtic Nature Prayers

Prayers from an Ancient Well

Kenneth McIntosh

Celtic Nature Prayers:
Prayers from an Ancient Well

Copyright © 2015 by Anamchara Books, a division of Harding House Publishing Service, Inc. All rights reserved. No part of this publication may be reproduced or transmitted in any form or by any means, electronic or mechanical, including photocopying, recording, taping, or any information storage and retrieval system, without permission from the publisher.

Anamchara Books
Vestal, NY 13850
www.anamcharabooks.com

IngramSpark ISBN: 978-1-62524-814-5

Bible quotations labeled KJV are from the King James Version of the Bible; quotations labeled DRT are from the Douay–Rheims translation of the Bible; quotations labeled NIV are from the Holy Bible, New International Version®, NIV® Copyright ©1973, 1978, 1984, 2011 by Biblica, Inc.® Used by permission. All rights reserved worldwide.

Contents

Introduction	7
1. Finding God in Nature	13
2. The Blessings of the Earth	55
3. Prayers for the Planet	95
4. Learning from Nature's Wisdom	113
5. Worshipping God in Nature	141
Sources	179

Introduction

Finding God in Nature is one of the strongest elements in both Christian and pagan Celtic spirituality. The Celts are not alone in this: the feeling of being closer to God in Nature seems to be instinctive, and many faith traditions see in Nature the revelation of its Maker. A Hindu teacher said, "Like rain in the river going back to the ocean, every drop of water that wants to go back to its source is a religious seeker." Poet Elizabeth Browning wrote, "Earth is crammed with heaven and every bush aflame with God," and Hebrew and Christian scriptures affirm this perspective; in Psalm 29, David likens a thunderstorm to God's voice: "The voice of the Lord is over the waters: the God of glory thunders. . . . The voice of the Lord twists the oaks and strips the forest bare."

Long before they had heard about Christianity, the Celts knew that Nature was their portal to a great spiritual reality. Wells, mountain crags, caves, and lochs were "thin places" that allowed access to the realm of spirits. In these temples of Nature, the Celts sought physical and spiritual healing, as well as revelation. The salmon, the eagle, and even the tiny hazelnut, all were allies in helping humanity access the mysterious magic that underlay physical matter.

The Celtic followers of Christ affirmed their ancestors' instincts. One of the most ancient Celtic catechisms, attributed to Saint Ninian, asked, "What is the fruit of study?" His answer: "To perceive the eternal Word of God reflected in every plant and insect, every bird and animal, every man and woman." John Scotus Erigena, an Irishman who lived at the beginning of the ninth century, believed all reality, including Nature, proceeds continually from God. "The whole of reality then is God," Erigena wrote, "since God is source, sustainer, and end." As Erigena's admirer, Christopher Bamford explains, "All things—human nature, the universe, each one of us—are divine lights, luminous theophanies. The universe, the human soul, is a vast light-filled discourse, every word of which is uttered in and by The Word."

The Celts had a fluid sense of history, one that was based more on a deep inner truth than on chronological accuracy—so although many of these prayers are not necessarily "historically accurate," they are all true to the Celtic spirit. The prayers collected here point our hearts toward the Celtic way of thinking about Nature, using rhythms and word patterns that reflect those that the ancient Celt would have used. Many of these prayers are from the *Carmina Gadelica*, a collection of old Scottish prayers gathered from primary sources by a nineteenth-century scholar named Alexander Carmicheal. Other prayers we've included here are from ancient Welsh or Irish sources. Many were inspired by older prayers, and some are completely modern creations of our own. (To find the author of each prayer, see the back of the book.) You'll find quotes from other sources as well, both mystics and modern authors, to provide a wider context for these Celtic Nature prayers. Our goal is not to give you a tool for knowing the ancient Celts—but rather a tool for knowing God! We hope this book will be useful in several different ways.

First, there are days when we don't have a prayer (literally). We're too banjaxed to come up with the words needed to connect with God—and those are the times that books of written prayers can be most useful. Sometimes they are just what we wanted to say if we could have only found the words.

We also hope these prayers will inspire you to speak even more freely with God using your own utterances. As a spark catches fire and spreads, so the prayers of others can enflame our tongues to form their own deeply personal and private prayers.

Above all, we hope you'll be encouraged to "pray without ceasing" as the Apostle Paul recommends. The Celtic way is to recognize God's presence woven into the knotwork of every day: good times or bad, success or failure, at our best or our worst. The Threefold God is always with us—and Celtic prayers are a way for us to be sure that we are conscious of the Divine presence.

Creator bless you
Christ bless you
Spirit bless you
Bless you threefold
Bless you head to toe
Bless you through these prayers.

1
Finding God in Nature

Do not I fill heaven and earth? saith the Lord.

Jeremiah 23:24 KJV

Not everyone senses God's presence in a church—but almost everyone has felt *something* while alone in Nature, some tickling inkling that Someone is there in the solitude. Personally, I have a special place I go to be alone with God. I ride my bike there, and the red-brown trunks and grey-green needles of Ponderosa pines fly past me as I steer my bike along the trail. The path meanders back and forth along a dry creek bed, then climbs uphill through rock formations where I have to gear down, stand on the pedals, and balance the bike. Finally, I descend into a meadow and reach my intended destination, my "prayer rock," the place I've named "Aslan's Throne." The volcanic rock is twice my height, pockmarked by time, and mottled with patches of lichen.

My mind tells me that my prayer rock's features are all the natural results of volcanic eruption and the erosion of wind and water, but it's hard not to see a Divine hand behind the shaping of this rock; it's a perfect outdoor sanctuary. And perhaps the Divine plan is even *more* miraculous when it takes a million years to work its way to fruition.

Atop this monumental stone, I fold my legs, turn my hands upward on my knees, and close my eyes. I feel I am rooted to the Earth, as solidly placed as the stone. I begin to pray, bringing to mind my friends, loved ones, people in need of various help, and the woes of the world. Then my thoughts turn to sheer thankfulness—for the forest, the sun, this rock . . . and then, my meditation moves past words. Presence embraces me. The stillness has become preternatural. I can no longer hear the ravens or the rustle of pines. I open my eyes and find the scene has shifted subtly: colors are brighter, lines crisper, and . . .

Somehow, I'm looking both from my eyes and simultaneously from beyond my point of view. "I" am no longer here. My body has merged with the Earth, the trees, and the sky. I am one with the forest and with God.

I'm not sure how long this reverie lasts, because time seems to have stopped. It's like being in a still photograph, only intensely tangible. I've entered into what seems like the very edge of God's view of the world, pulled outside space and time.

Spiritual masters from many religious traditions emphasize that we all need to find moments when we escape the world's busyness. Alone, in silence, we can begin to hear the Voice. As Mahatma Gandhi put it, "The divine radio is always singing if we could only make ourselves ready to listen to it, but it is impossible to listen without silence." Nature's quiet places offer us that silence where we can hear God's voice.

Prayer Rock

Lord of the forest trail,
of the winding wooded way,
I thank You for this sacred space;

Through creek bed,
over meadow and hill,
I worship Creator God,
and I thank You for this sacred space.
For a fall chill this bright morning,
for gray-green needle of the pine,
I thank You.

Seeking the secret place, my rock
I worship Jesus, friend.

Sitting in the stillness, body one with stone
    I worship Spirit, true.

    Body one with earth and tree,
    I worship now the blessed three
      in forest, hill, and rock.

    Raven calls, breaking silence,
      calling me to go.
    but as I leave, stay with me.
    As I leave, be with me.
    Bless the winding, wooded way
      to my soul.

God in All Things

Thou art the joy of all joyous things,
Thou art the light of the beam of the sun,
Thou art the door of the chief of hospitality,
Thou art the field of plenty,
Thou art the surpassing star of guidance,
Thou art the step of the deer in the wood,
Thou art the step of the steed on the plain,
Thou art the grace of the swan a-swimming,
Thou art the loveliness of all lovely desires.

*The essence of Divinity
is found in every single thing. . . .
Do not say,
"This is a stone and not God."
God forbid!
Rather, all existence is God,
and the stone is a thing pervaded by Divinity.*

Moses Cordovero

The Song of Amergin

Amergin was the legendary Bard of the Milesian people at the time when they settled in Ireland. The composition of this poem hearkens to the pre-Christian past and reminds us that the Celts had a concept of the Divine Spirit in nature even before they heard of Christ.

> I am the wind on the sea.
> I am the ocean wave.
> I am the sound of the billows.
> I am the seven-horned stag.
> I am the hawk on the cliff.
> I am the dewdrop in sunlight.

I am the fairest of flowers.
I am the raging boar.

I am the salmon in the deep pool.
I am the lake on the plain.
I am the meaning of the poem.
I am the point of the spear.
I am the god that makes fire in the head.
Who levels the mountain?
Who speaks the age of the moon?
Who has been where the sun sleeps?
Who?
If not I?

A Simple Touch

Lord, I only need
a simple touch today:

a ray of sun,
or drop of rain,
coo of dove,
rustling leaf,
water cleansing my face,
cat brushing my leg,
warm mug in hand,
solid ground under foot.

In the simple
You are here
loving me today.

The Likeness of the Lord

Thou art the joy of all joyous things,
Thou art the light of the beam of the sun.
Thou art the surpassing star of guidance,
Thou art the step of the deer of the hill,
Thou art the step of the steed of the plain,
Thou art the grace of the swan of swimming,
Thou art the loveliness of all lovely desires.
The lovely likeness of the Lord
is in loveliness
everywhere upon the earth.

King of All Nature

Thou King of the moon,
Thou King of the sun,
Thou King of the planets,
Thou King of the stars,
Thou King of the globe,
Thou King of the sky,
Oh! lovely Thy countenance,
Thou beauteous Beam.

God of the Moon, God of the Sun

God of the moon, God of the sun,
God of the globe, God of the stars,
God of the waters, the land, and the skies,
who ordained to us the King of promise.
It was Mary fair who went upon her knee,
it was the King of life who went upon her lap,
darkness and tears were set behind,
and the star of guidance went up early.
illumined the land, illumined the world,
Illumined doldrum and current.
Grief was laid and joy was raised.

The Hermit's Song

I wish, O Son of the living God,
O ancient, eternal King,
For a hidden little hut in the wilderness
that it may be my dwelling.
An all-grey lithe little lark to be by its side,
A clear pool to wash away sins
through the grace of the Holy Spirit.
Quite near, a beautiful wood
around it on every side,
To nurse many-voiced birds,
hiding it with its shelter.
A southern aspect for warmth,
a little brook across its floor,
A choice land with many gracious gifts
such as be good for every plant.

Prayer of the Green Place

Alone, in this green place,
I am seeing with the eye of the One
who created me;
I am filled with the love of the One
who died for me;
I am breathing with the breath of the Spirit
who breathes in me.

Grant to me, Lord of the Green Place,
awareness of Your Presence.
May I take with me the awareness I have here
when I return to my busy life.

As I drive on highways,
sit in front of a computer screen,
talk with coworkers, friends, and family,
and go about my daily tasks,
keep in my heart a quiet green place
where I can go,
a place where
I will see with the eye of the One
who created me;
be filled with the love of the One
who died for me;
and breathe with the breath of the Spirit
who breathes in me.

The Healing of Empty Places

God, alone by the sea,
I feel Your wildness in the waves.
Alone by a quiet lake,
I see Your peace in the calm water.
Alone in the forest,
I hear Your voice in the leaves.
Alone in the desert,
I breathe Your fierce heat in the air.
Come, I pray, to me in these empty places
and heal my heart.

God's Presence

You are the peace of morning calm.
You are the tree that shelters from harm.
You are the stars that shine in the dark.
You are the heart's eternal spark.
You are the spring that brings new life.
You are the cold that cuts like a knife.
You are the fox that barks in the night.
You are the mountain's lofty height.

You are in soil and air,
and flowing stream,
in fog's grey damp
and gold sunbeam.
I walk on the Earth,
and find Your way
in Nature's breath, constant each day,
In scent of leaf and growing seed.
You come anew and meet my need.

*The world is God's letter to human beings.
Divine thoughts are flashing upon us
from every direction.*

Plato

NIGHT

God of the stars, shelter me from harm.
God of the moon, shelter me from fear.
God of the dark, shelter me from troubling thoughts.
God of the night sound, shelter me in peace.
God of the cool breeze, shelter me in sleep.

Prayer of the New Moon

In name of the Holy Spirit of grace,
In name of the Father of the City of peace,
In name of Jesus who took death off us,
Oh! in name of the Three who shield us in every need,
If well thou hast found us tonight,
Seven times better mayest thou leave us without
harm,
Thou bright white Moon of the seasons,
Bright white Moon of the seasons.

Morning

In the darkness-fleeing day,
in the dawning light
with the cooing dove of morn,
I walk with Creator God

Twig snaps under foot,
leaf rustles, grass whispers,
and in the morning light,
I walk with my King.

The meadow alive with buzzing bee,
flowers sway in cooling breeze,
in the soft start of day,
I walk with the Spirit Holy

O Three in One,
bless the raven, dove, and sparrows,
and bless my heart
in this morning walk
into a new day.

Look No Farther

Your living face,
Lord of Life and Love,
is in earth and sea,
in sky and creature,
everywhere.
No words contain You.
No thought defines You.
But You are everywhere,
in earth and sea,
in sky and creature.
I need look no farther

Has God any dwelling-place
save earth and sea,
the air of heaven and virtuous hearts?
Why seek the Deity further?
Whatever we see is God.

Lucan

God's Song

I am the amoeba swimming in pond water.
I am the elephant stepping gently on huge feet.
I am the whale that sings its song
seven fathoms deep.
I am the chickadee with dark bright eye.
I am the hawk rising swift on currents of wind.
I am the tiger stalking its prey.
I am the platypus,
most confused of all animals.
I am the wild goose flying on strong winds.
I am the rabbit,
fleet of foot and timid of heart.

I am the minnow, darting in shallow water;
the tadpole transforming into something new;
the caterpillar never dreaming of wings;
the butterfly that speaks to you of resurrection;
the cat curled in your lap;
the spider spinning her web;
the cow, patient servant of humanity;
and the cricket, singing its autumn song.
I am the breath of each one.
I am the Spirit in each.
Look.
I am everywhere you turn,
if you only had eyes to see.

Every visible or invisible creature
is a theophany,
a manifestation of God.

John Scotus Erigena

God's Hand Held Out

May the Earth rise up to meet your soles,
that with each step you take,
you might feel the Holy beneath your feet.
May you feel the wind on your face,
and know it is your Mother's breath.
May the rain fall soft on you,
opening your heart to know,
that the Earth is the palm of God's hand,
held out to you in love.

Grasp the Creator through Creation,
seeing God reflected in created things
as the sun is reflected in water

Saint Theodoric

CHRIST IN CREATURES

I saw Christ today,
hungry
outside my windows in the winter cold,
and I filled my birdfeeders
that He might be filled.
I saw Christ today,
running on swift hooves across the road,
and I slowed my car that He might be safe.
I saw Christ today,
in the glad face of my dog,
as I greeted her at the end of the workday.

I saw Christ today,
in the moth that beat against the window,
until I let it out into the night.
Each time I saw Christ,
He blessed me,
in the Holy Name of the Trinity,
and the bird outside my window sang
again and again,
"Often and often, goes Christ
on wing and hoof and paw."

Even when my Beloved is not in my thoughts,
He is never absent from my sight,
because everything I see
is a picture of my Beloved.

Ramon Lull

Open My Ears

Give me ears to hear,
Your voice speaking
through woodchuck and wolverine,
crow and coyote,
herring and humming bird.
Teach me to listen.

*Every creature is a divine word
because it proclaims God.*

Saint Bonaventure

Open My Eyes

Give me eyes to see You,
strong in the oak tree;
constant in the mountains;
ever green in fir and pine;
playful in otter;
swift in cheetah paws;
gentle in giraffes;
humble in earthworm;
proud in lion and lynx;
flowing in bright stream;
soft in bird feathers;
and solid in stone.

*Open your eyes
and the whole world is full of God.*

Jacob Boehme

God Is Speaking

You are speaking to me
through the ocean's waves,
whispering, "Peace";
You are singing joy
from a robin's throat;
my dog's wagging tail
is Your tale of love;
and You are promising forever
in spring's new buds.

Believe one who knows:
you will find something greater in woods
than in books.
Trees and stones will teach you
that which you can never learn from masters.

Saint Bernard de Clairvaux

Hymn to the Presence of God

Fiery Creator of fire,

Giver of light,

Life and Author of life,

Salvation and Bestower of Salvation,

I see You in fire,

in light,

in all of life.

I cannot see Your face,

I am blind,

wandering in the dark,

yet You speak promises to me

in cloud, in starlight,

in moon and sun.

You call out to me
in morning light,
in light that ripples on water,
on candlelight that glimmers in darkness.
Though You are a consuming fire,
You do not burn what You illumine.
I taste Your sweetness
in the recesses of the bee's comb.
The sweet food of Your honey
fills the inmost cells of my heart,
and I am filled.
The bees swarm into the air;
may, I like them, win heaven
on wings now free from care.

Has God any dwelling-place
save earth and sea,
the air of heaven and virtuous hearts?
Why seek the Deity further?
Whatever we see is God.

Lucan

2
The Blessings of the Earth

The universe has become an ocean of blessings.

Saint Clement of Alexandria

Some of the most beautiful Celtic prayers are benedictions that call upon the forces of Nature, guided by God's presence within them, to bless each person. These prayers were not so much prayers *to* Nature as they were expressions of the Celts' belief that God's hand moved within Nature.

The idea of the Earth as a living being—a loving, nurturing female being—has a long tradition. The early Greeks worshipped the goddess Gaia as the personification of the Earth, while the Romans' version of the same goddess was Terra. The indigenous faiths of nearly every culture have had a similar goddess, including the Pagan Celts. Today, we speak lightly of Mother Nature, but few of us relate to her with the awe and reverence that pre-Christian cultures felt. However, a modern theory, the Gaia hypothesis, proposes a scientific version of this concept, describing Earth as an integrated whole, a complex, self-regulating system that maintains all life on our planet.

Today, one of the challenges spiritual people face is to integrate their faith with a living relationship to the Earth. Unfortunately, many forms of Christianity have regarded the Earth as the source of sin and temptation, the exact opposite of the spiritual world where God dwells. Ecotheologian Thomas Berry writes that we need a new "awareness that the mountains and rivers and all living things, the sky and its sun and moon and clouds all constitute a healing, sustaining sacred presence for humans which they need as much for their psychic integrity as for their physical nourishment." We cannot separate our "earthly lives" from our "spiritual lives," says Berry. "In our totality we are born of the earth. . . . The earth is our origin, our nourishment, our support, our guide. Our spirituality itself is earth-derived."

The Christian Celts give us a model for living out a faith that is rooted in the Earth. When they turned to Christianity, they no longer worshipped their old gods and goddesses—but their new faith was wide enough to absorb their sense that the Earth was a living, nurturing expression of the Divine. Recognizing God's Presence in soil and sky, the turning seasons, in beasts and plants, they continued to relate to the Earth with love and wonder. And they felt great gratitude for the many blessings—Divine blessings—the Earth bestowed.

The Earth's Blessings

When you feel the sun's light upon you,
may you be lit within your heart,
so that friends and strangers
will come and warm themselves,
as though a fire burned within you.
When you look up at the bright sky,
may its light enter you
and shine out from your two eyes,
like candles in the windows of a house,
showing the way to those who are lost.

When the cold rain falls on you,
may you feel its blessing,
so that it beats upon your spirit,
washing it fair and clean,
leaving within you a shining pool
that reflects the blue of Heaven,
and sometimes a star.
May the Earth bless you each day,
so that your heart is strengthened.
May you trust her as you trust God,
so that one day you will not be afraid
to give your body to her,
knowing she will keep you safe
until the day of your rising.

Come forth into the light of things,
Let Nature be your teacher.

William Wordsworth

Prayer of Blessing

God's peace be to you,
Jesus' peace be to you,
Spirit's peace be to you
Earth's peace to you,
and to your children.
My own blessing be with you.
The blessing of God be with you.
The blessing of Jesus be with you.
The blessing of Spirit be with you.
The blessing of Earth be with you,
and with your children.

May God shield you on every steep,
May Christ aid you on every path,
May Spirit fill you on every slope.
May you find blessings on field and plain.
May the King shield you in the valleys,
May Christ aid you on the mountains,
May Spirit bathe you on the slopes.
in hollow, on hill, mountain, valley, and plain,
may you see writ the shape of Christ.

The shape of Christ be before you.
The shape of Christ be behind you.
The shape of Christ be over you.
The shape of Christ be under you.
The shape of Christ be with you.
The shape of Christ be around you.
In wind and cloud, light and rain,
in fog and chill, in sun and heat,
may you see writ the shape of Christ.

A Child's Blessing

I bathe your palms with rainwater,
that your spirit may always be refreshed.
I bathe your eyes in starfire,
that your imagination may be kindled.
I bathe your limbs in the sap of mighty trees,
that you may have strength
for each day that lies ahead.
I bless your face with the pattern
of leaves against the sky,
that you may always recognize beauty.

I bless your hands
with the touch of fur and feather,
that you may have tenderness
for those who are smaller than you.
I bless your lips
with the taste of fruit and grain,
that you may know the Earth
is the source of your nourishment.
I give you the integrity of cattle,
the swiftness of hawk wings,
and the sweetness of spring blossoms.
May the Earth bless your coming;
may she bless your growing;
and may she bless you
all the days of your life.

If you wish your children to think deep thoughts,
to know the holiest emotions,
take them to the woods and hills,
and give them the freedom of the meadows;
the hills purify those who walk upon them.

Richard Jefferies

Cradle Song

Sleep, my babe, lie still and slumber,
God's guardian angels without number,
fly among the stars so bright.
all through the night.
The Earth shelters you,
you'll not be lonely,
for angels aren't your guardian only.

Tree and hill standing tall,
vines that creep upon the wall,
all are whispering out your name,
all are guarding you from harm.
Soft and drowsy hours are creeping,
each leaf and flower in slumber sleeping,
while owls watch are keeping,
all through the night.
Night's dark shades need hold no fear,
for friendly creatures hover near,
and God loves you dear,
all through the night.

Your deepest roots are in nature.
No matter who you are, where you live,
or what kind of life you lead,
you remain irrevocably linked
with the rest of creation.

Charles Cook

A Prayer for a Friend

May the blessing of light be on you—
the warm light of the sun,
the silver light of the moon,
the light of stars and running water,
and the light of God within your heart.
May the blessed light shine on you
and warm your heart
till it glows like a great peat fire.
May you see God's light on the path ahead
when the road you walk is dark.

May you always hear,
even in your hour of sorrow,
the sweet song of a bird outside your window.
When trouble comes,
may the summer rain be gentle on you,
and your heart not turn to stone.
Take comfort in the simple blessings
of fertile earth and shining sky,
and know through every sigh
you do not walk alone.

*After all, I don't see why
I am always asking for private,
individual, selfish miracles
when every year there are miracles
like white dogwood.*

Anne Morrow Lindbergh

CLOUDS

The clouds I see, Christ sees;
On this journey I walk, he walks.
May the Three of Heaven protect me here.
and each man, woman, and child.
Shade us from heat and drought,
O Holy Cloud.
Give water to the ewe and the lamb.
May all I meet give welcome
and every path be open.
Clouds above me, Christ above me,
all the way.
O nourish me to the end
till my last threshold I cross o'er.

Irish Benediction

Many Celtic blessings were given at leave-taking, calling on Nature's protection for loved ones as they traveled.

May the road rise to meet you,
May the wind be always at your back.
May the sun shine warm upon your face,
The rains fall soft upon your fields.
And until we meet again,
May God hold you in the palm of his hand.

May green be the grass you walk on,
May blue be the skies above you,
May pure be the joys that surround you,
May true be the hearts that love you.

The Earth's Deep Peace

Deep peace I breathe into you,
O weariness, here:
O ache, here!
Deep peace, a soft white dove to you;
deep peace, a quiet rain to you;
deep peace, an ebbing wave to you!
Deep peace, red wind of the east from you;
deep peace, grey wind of the west to you;
deep peace, dark wind of the north from you;
deep peace, blue wind of the south to you!

Deep peace, pure red of the flame to you;
deep peace, pure white of the moon to you;
deep peace, pure green of the grass to you;
deep peace, pure brown of the earth to you;
deep peace, pure grey of the dew to you;
deep peace, pure blue of the sky to you!

Deep peace of the running wave to you;
deep peace of the flowing air to you;
deep peace of the quiet earth to you;
deep peace of the sleeping stones to you!

Deep peace of the shining stars to you;
deep peace of infinite space to you;
deep peace from the Son of Peace to you!
Deep peace from the heart of Mary to you,
and from Brigid of the Mantle
deep peace, deep peace!

And with the kindness
of the Heavenly Father, peace!
In the name of the Three
who are One, peace!

And by the will of the One
who rules wind and rain,
storm and sun,
the moon, the hills,
and all the Earth's round globe,
peace! Peace!

Thanksgiving

We return thanks to our mother,
the Earth, who sustains us.
We return thanks to the rivers and streams,
which supply us with water.
We return thanks to all herbs,
which furnish medicines for the cure of our diseases.
We return thanks to the moon and stars,
which have given to us their light.
We return thanks to the sun,
who has looked upon the Earth with a friendly eye.
Lastly, we return thanks to the Great Spirit,
in Whom is embodied all goodness,
and Who directs all things for good.

If there is any wisdom
running through my life now,
in my walking on this earth,
it came from listening in the Great Silence
to the stones, trees, space, the wild animals,
to the pulse of all life as my heartbeat.

Vijali Hamilton

COME I THIS DAY

Come I this day to the forest,
come I this day to the field,
come I this day to the mountains,
come I this day to seaside and river.
I find in each place
the Creator, the Son, and the Spirit,
filled with power and kindly balm
to ease and heal my soul.
God and Spirit and Jesus,
from the crown of my head
to the soles of my feet,
give to me the Earth's blessing.

Come I with my reputation,
come I with my work,
come I with all my words,
come I with all I love.
Come I this day with God,
come I this day with Christ,
come I with the Spirit,
here, in these quiet places.
Come I to You, Jesu.
Jesu, shelter me.

I Have No Need of a Kingdom

I have no need of a kingdom,
no need of any home but the Earth.
The blackbird sings as beautiful
as any human voice.
Grazing deer, a badger's brood,
foxes to meet them in peace,
and all that is delightful
give me more pleasure
than any walls of wood and stone.

The Blessings of the Earth

An apple tree is ready like an inn;
a thick little bush with fistfuls of hazel-nuts;
green, full of branches;
a rowan tree, a sloe bush;
dark black thorns, plenty of food;
acorns, haws, yew berries; bearberries, blueberries:
better than any meal.

Buzzing of bees,
the cackle of wild geese before the winter;
the voice of the wind against the branches;
that is delightful music.
And this is all I need.
I have no need of a kingdom.

As long as I live,
I'll hear waterfalls and birds and winds sing.
I'll interpret the rocks,
learn the language of flood,
storm, and the avalanche.
I'll acquaint myself
with the glaciers and wild gardens,
and get as near
to the heart of the world as I can.

John Muir

A Small Place
in the Wilderness

I wish, O Son of the Living God,
O ancient and eternal King,
for a hidden small place in the wilderness.
There I would live.
The grayest wren, lithe and small,
would live there too.
A clear pool would be there,
Earth's water to wash away all brokenness,
by the grace of Your Bright Spirit.
The woods would surround me,
many-voiced birds sheltering within it.

The sun for my warmth,
and a little brook nearby;
land filled with the Earth's choice gifts
to nourish every plant.
This would be my church, a dwelling for God,
a shining candle like the pure-white Scriptures.
This would be the house
where I would flee when my body is tired,
a place without boasting,
without shallow emotion,

without thought of evil.
I would care for this land,
and it would nourish me
with fragrant leeks, salmon, trout, and bees.
The Earth would give me all I need,
food and clothing
from the King of Heaven and Earth.
And I would sit there praying to God,
and I would bring it with me in every place
so that it never left my heart.

Thousands of tired, nerve-shaken,
over-civilized people
are beginning to find out
that going to the mountains is going home;
that wildness is a necessity.

John Muir

BLESSINGS EVERYWHERE

The oak tree blesses me,
O God of strength.
The stone in my hand blesses me,
O God who endures.
The bird on the wing blesses me,
O God of freedom.
The deer in the forest blesses me,
O God of gentleness.

The abundance of bluebells on the hills
blesses me,
O God of bounty.
Starlight and moonlight bless me,
O God of quiet illumination.
The wind in the trees blesses me,
O God of Spirit-Breath.
The rain on my face blesses me,
O God who cleanses me.
Each thing I see blesses me,
O God who loves me.

St. Patrick's Breastplate

I arise today

Through the strength of heaven:

Light of sun,

Radiance of moon,

Splendour of fire,

Speed of lightning,

Swiftness of wind,

Depth of sea,

Stability of earth,

Firmness of rock.

Rain

Bless to me, O God,
this gentle rain tonight.
Bless to me, O God,
this sound that brings me sleep.
Bless to me, O God,
fresh scents that fill the air,
my warm and cozy home,
the feeling that You're near,
the knowledge that this rain tonight
brings life for earth tomorrow.

A Chant for Columba's Plant

Gaelic people in old times had chants for everything they did during the day. The plant in this refrain—Columba's plant—is what we now call Saint John's wort. In the Dark Ages and in the Middle Ages, this plant was believed to have the power to drive away evil. Today, we know that St. John's wort can be used as an antidepressant. This prayer reminds us that all is holy—plants, medicines, chemicals—and can carry God's blessings to us.

> I will pluck what I meet,
> as in communion with my saint,
> to stop the wiles of wily men,
> and the arts of foolish women.

I will pluck my Columba plant,
as a prayer to my King,
that mine be the power of Columba's plant,
over every one I see.
I will pluck the leaf above,
as ordained of the High King,
in name of the Three of Glory

3
Prayers for the Planet

*For the creation waits in eager expectation
. . . in hope that the creation itself
will be liberated from its bondage.*

Romans 8:19,21 NIV

Many modern Christians have fallen prey to bifurcated thinking: they see ecology as having no ongoing role in Christian life. On the other hand, others say, "I don't need to go to church—I worship while I'm alone in the woods, by the ocean, or in the desert." In both cases, Christian practice and the natural world have been artificially separated.

For the ancient Celts, this split between their Christian selves and their nature-loving selves would have been impossible; the two aspects of their lives were like strands of a single rope. Christ the Divine Logos equally revealed God to humanity through the scriptures, in the wilderness, in the meeting of God's people, and out on the ocean. Restoring a parched field to arability was an act of worship, and the rituals of the church underscored the importance of the Earth. As Philip Newell, former Warden of Iona and Celtic spiritual writer, puts it, "In the ancient Celtic mission, from the fourth to seventh centuries, the pattern for worship was to gather around high-standing crosses in the context of earth, sea, and sky. The emphasis was that creation itself was the Sanctuary of God. And it included all things."

We have torn the sacred from the Earth with disastrous consequences. Science and religion engage in bitter debates, though both are ways to understand the Mystery that is God. Ecology and biblical theology are set in opposition, though ecology is service to God's very Being. Many people see God and Jesus as obsolete and irrelevant—if not destructive—in a world beset by scarce resources, global warming, and ecological collapse.

We need to rediscover how "to perceive the eternal Word of God reflected in every plant and insect, every bird and animal, every man and woman" (in the words of Ninian's Catechism). Faith in Jesus and trust in God could empower more good on behalf of our world than we can imagine. It could mend the broken bridges between ourselves and our planet, bringing into being the active reconciliation are world so desperately needs.

LADY EARTH

I am bowing my head
in the eye of the Mother
who gave me birth,
in the eye of the Father
who loves me,
in the eye of the Spirit
who guides me in wisdom,
in friendship and affection
within Nature's green places.
O loving God,
bestow upon us fullness in our need.
Grant us love for Lady Earth,
that we in turn may be blessed
with her affection.

Your laughter ringing with hers,
Your wisdom woven with hers,
Your blessing working
in her and on her,
our Lady Earth,
doing Your will here
as the Ageless Ones do in Heaven.
Each shade and light,
each day and night,
each moment in kindness,
grant us Your sight
to see the blessings held out to us
from Lady Earth.

GREAT SPIRIT PRAYER

Give us hearts to understand,
never to take from creation's beauty
more than we give;
Never to hold back our hands
from rebuilding the Earth's beauty;
never to take from her what we cannot use.
Give us hearts to understand
that as we care for her,
she will care for us.

THE SHIELD OF GOD

God of Heaven, God of Earth,
hold Your shield over us, protect us all,
Jesu beloved!
Creator of the Shining Ones!
Shield, oh shield us
in the arms of the Earth.
Safeguard our animals,
the small ones we love,
encircle us together.
You walk the trackways of power
across the Earth,
You guide the stars.

Guide well ourselves,
and shield, we pray,
the great and ancient procession
of life across Your Earth.
O Creator! O Father!
O Mother! O Christ!
O Spirit! O Wisdom!
Be the Triad with us day and night,
on fertile field and rocky mountain ridge.
Be the Triad who is One

and wrap Earth's cloak of air around us.
May we feel Your shield
in snowfall and winter gloom,
in green buds and springtime joy,
in the heat of summer days
and in autumn's sweet abundance.
Be with us in each one
and wrap Your love around us.
O Three in One,
wrap Your love around us.

Beltane Blessing

Beltane is May Day, the beginning of Celtic summer.

Bless, O Threefold true and bountiful,
myself, my spouse, and my children,
on the fragrant plain, on the mountain wild place,
on the fragrant plain, on the mountain wild place.
Everything within my dwelling or in my possession,
all kine and crops, all flocks and corn,
from Hallow Eve to Beltane Eve,
with goodly progress and gentle blessing,
from sea to sea, and every river mouth,
from wave to wave, and base of waterfall.
And shield these loved ones beneath Thy wing of glory,

shield my loved ones beneath the wing of Thy glory.
Bless everything and every one,
place the cross of Christ on us
with the power of love,
till we see the land of joy,
till we see the land of joy.
May the tending of the Triune follow all beasts;
may the tending of the Triune follow them.
Thou Being who didst create me at the beginning,
listen and attend me as I bend the knee to Thee,
morning and evening as is becoming in me,
in Thine own presence, O God of life,
in Thine own presence, O God of life.

BLESSING FOR THE REAPING

God, bless Thou Thyself
each ridge, and plain, and field,
safeguard them beneath thy shield of strength,
and guard them in the house of the saints,
guard them in the house of the saints.
Encompass each living creature,
and tend them to a kindly fold.
Tend them to a kindly fold
for the sake of Michael head of hosts,
of Mary fair-skinned branch of grace,
of Bride smooth-white of ringleted locks,
of Columba of the graves and tombs,
Columba of the graves and tombs.

A Prayer of Protection for the Earth

O Threefold Maker of Wonders,
as Thou art the Spirit within all things green
guard Thou the air-giving forests,
curb those who belch toxic emissions.
Thou Shield of Protection, guard us forever
Be Thou a force of strong conscience
to shield us securely from destroying the Earth,
from the corporations and the need to exploit,
and from our own greedy natures.
O Thou who sustains the very air we breathe,
as Thou art the Spirit in all things green,
save us from our folly.
Call us to Thy aid.

St. Basil's Prayer of Compassion

O God, enlarge within us
the sense of fellowship with all living things,
our brothers the animals
to whom Thou gave the Earth
as their home in common with us.
We remember with shame that in the past
we have exercised our high dominion
with ruthless cruelty
so that the voice of the Earth,
which should have gone up to Thee in song,
has been a groan of travail.
May we realize that they live not for us alone
but for themselves and for Thee,
and that they love the sweetness of life.

Prayer for a Wounded Earth

God who is Three-in-One,
we know You see the sparrow fall.
Surely, You see each polar bear that dies
as Earth's polar ice melts.
Christ who is the Lamb slain,
surely You feel the pain of dolphins,
rhinos, gorillas, whales, and turtles,
dying from the wounds
we have dealt Your world.
God who is Mercy,
forgive us for our sins
against Your world.

Give us eyes to see
that as we wounded the Earth,
we have wounded You
with our greed and ignorance.
Give us strength to change.
Bless each beast, bird, and fish,
each plant and tree,
each insect and microbe,
and each human
within Your web of life.
Heal our wounds,
we pray.

Prayer for the Earth During Climate Change

We pray, O Three-in-One,
for a world of rising temperatures,
drought and flood,
wild weather and broken seasons,
failed crops and dying forests.
Creator God, in Your mercy,
renew this damaged world.
For each creature threatened by climate change,
we pray, O Three-in-One.
Creator God, in Your mercy,
renew this damaged world.

You who made the Earth,
remake her now.
Give us love and strength
to partner with You
and renew this damaged world

4
Learning from Nature's Wisdom

Nature does not hurry,
yet everything is accomplished.

Lao Tzu

Most modern men and women (at least in developed nations) live unnaturally separated from the planet that is our home. We can ignore the summer's scorching heat if we stay inside where there is air conditioning; we can ignore the winter's numbing cold while the thermostat keeps the heater running. Darkness is conquered by electric light and shades keep out unwanted glare.

None of us would wish to return to a more primitive life where we would be exposed to these elements; it's crazy to over-romanticize the pre-technology past. Yet we also lose something in this divorce from Earth's natural rhythms. Our bodies seem at times to struggle against us, for something innate and primal knows what season it is, and knows whether we should be hibernating for winter or dashing through the forests in spring, and even whether the moon is waxing and waning.

The ancient Celts, by contrast, lived almost entirely by the rhythm of Nature's cycles. Day and night changed slowly with each rotation of the Earth as sunrise and sunset grew closer together or further apart. The calendar was set by the solstices, equinoxes, and the four "cross-quarter" seasonal celebrations set between those four astronomical events (Imbolc, Beltane, Lughnasadh, and Samhain).

Activities—both labor and recreation—followed strictly the dictates of Nature. There was time to plant and time to gather, time to oversee the birthing and time for slaughtering, seasons to venture into deep waters and times to stay close to the shore. Likewise, the celebrations and gatherings of clans followed the dance of moon, sun, and stars. Even the cultivation of one's spiritual life followed the seasonal patterns: wintertime to huddle and contemplate, moving slowly and carefully at the spiritual level; springtime to dare and begin new audacious ventures.

While thankful for the convenience of modern controlled environments, we can learn from the ancient Celts and regain a mindful connection with the greater forces: the Earth, moon, and stars; day and night; wind, rain, and sunshine. As we learn from the Earth's wisdom, reclaiming our own relationships with both stillness and action, with death and darkness as well as life and light, we will become more at ease with the natural rhythms of our lives. Not every season is meant for fruit—so we need not be discouraged by barren times; creative periods of action must be preceded by quiet times of rest—and so we have no need for anxiety during the times when we feel as though circumstances have removed us from life's active flow. Nature's cycles of cloud and sun, summer and winter, day and night have many things to teach us.

Messages from God

As the rain hides the stars,
as the autumn mist
hides the hills,
as the clouds veil
the blue of the sky,
so the dark happenings of my life
hide the shining of Your face from me.
Yet the stars still shine behind the rain,
the hills are solid beneath the mist,
and when the wind drives the clouds away,
I see again the blue of Heaven.

As Your Earth reminds me
again and yet again
in all her changes
and in the wheel of her seasons,
You live beyond the momentary appearance
of my dark life.
Earth carries Your message to me,
and it is enough,
for though I may stumble in my going,
You will not fall.

*God writes the gospel
not in the Bible alone,
but on trees and flowers
and clouds and stars.*

Martin Luther

The Seasons

Spring clothes the Earth with flowers.
Lord, clothe me too in innocence.
Summer clothes the Earth in green.
Lord, clothe me too with life.
Autumn clothes the Earth with harvest bounty.
Lord, clothe me too with contentment.
Winter clothes the Earth in death.
Lord, strip everything from me,
but may I not forget
that spring always follows winter.

Climb the mountains
and get their good tidings.
Nature's peace will flow into you
as sunshine flows into trees.
The winds will blow their own freshness into you,
and the storms their energy,
while cares will drop off like autumn leaves.
. . . Nature's sources never fail.

John Muir

Heaven and Earth Are One

Watch the sun arise today
in mighty strength.
Let its beams reveal to you
Heaven's light.
Be upheld by soil and tree,
beast and river.
Here God's word in wind and water.
See God's shield in mount and plain.
Find God's path in Nature's seasons.
Whenever you walk in forest and field,
know that angels walk beside you,
for Heaven and Earth are one.

Seen with the eyes of contemplation,
a thistle has celestial qualities;
a speckled hen a touch of the divine.
Our greater comrades,
the trees, the clouds, the rivers,
initiate us into mighty secrets,
flame out at us.

Evelyn Underhill

Today's Work

Today, I will do my day's work
as would Mary, mother of Jesus,
never forgetting to look up and see the sky.
I will travel to my next place
in the presence of the angels,
seeing their wings among the trees.
Who is near me when I am sad and alone?
It is Jesus, the King of the sun,
who breathes His love on the wind
and sings comfort
in every sparrow's song.

Our planet gives us all things:
not only food and water,
but also the very structure of our lives,
days and nights, the seasons of the year,
these are Earth's gifts too.
May we learn to be aware,
so that at each sunrise, each nightfall,
we thank God.

Elizabeth Magid

Ebb and Flow

With the ebb, with the flow
of sea and tide,
teach me Thy patience.
Teach me that as it was,
as it is, as it shall be
evermore,
are all an ebb and flow
of Thy grace.
With the ebb, with the flow,
of earth and sea,
Remind me, O Thou Triune,
that Thy grace has no need of hurry.
With the ebb, with the flow,
so shall it be
evermore.

Adopt the pace of nature:
her secret is patience.

Ralph Waldo Emerson

FLY FREE

May the good Earth be soft under you
as you walk each day with God.
May you hold the Earth's blessings
with open hands.
May your hand rest so lightly
on the good Earth,
that when you lie at last
beneath her,
she will in turn rest so lightly on you
that your soul will fly free,
up and off
on its way to God
who never left you.

Shall I not have intelligence with the earth?
Am I not partly leaves
and vegetable mould
myself?

Henry David Thoreau

Prayer at a Loved One's Death

As you leave us
to go into a place we cannot see,
may you be as free as the wind is free,
may your way be soft as sheep's wool,
may your journey be as a hawk's,
flying straight into the heart of God.
At birth, you were immersed in water.
Now we immerse you into the life of God.
We entrust you to the Earth,
that she may receive you
as a mother receives into her arms
her tired child.

And then, may kindly Michael,
chief of the holy angels,
take charge of your beloved soul,
and bring it home
to the Three of All-Love:
Creator, Savior, Eternal Spirit,
world without end.
Amen

*All that live must die,
passing through Nature
into Eternity.*

William Shakespeare

The Archangels' Blessings on the Days

On the Earth's Sunday,
may I see Gabriel
and the power of the King of Heaven.
Gabriel be always with me
that evil may not come to me nor injury.

On the Earth's Monday,
my mind is set on Michael.
I can compare him to no one
but Jesus, the son of Mary.

On the Earth's Tuesday,
I call to Raphael for help.
He is one of the seven I beseech
as long as I am in the world's pasture.

On the Earth's Wednesday, may Uriel—
abbot of great nobility—be with me,
protecting me from danger and wound,
against wave and wind.

On the Earth's Thursday, I speak of Sariel,
who guards against storm,
and every evil I face
every disease that might seize me.

On the day of the Earth's Friday,
I give my love to Rumiel as my friend,
on the day when the Crucifixion
is writ forever into Time.

As long as I am on the green world,
so long as I live in the yellow world of air,
may Panchel be with me
on all the Saturdays I live.

In each space between,
in the darkness of night,
keep me safe with You, O Lord,
in the eternal kingdom,
where there is flaming radiance for ever.

On each day of sun and cloud,
may the Trinity protect me!
In each night of dark,
may the Trinity defend me!
May the Trinity save me from every hurt,
from every danger!

Earth, Teach Me

Earth, teach me humility
as blossoms are humble with beginning.
Earth, teach me courage
as the tree which stands alone.
Earth, teach me limitation
as the ant which crawls on the ground.
Earth, teach me freedom
as the eagle which soars in the sky.
Earth, teach me regeneration
as the seed which rises in the spring.
Earth, teach me to forget myself
as melted snow forgets its life.

Those who contemplate
the beauty of the earth
find reserves of strength that will endure
as long as life lasts.
There is something infinitely healing
in the repeated refrains of nature—
the assurance that dawn comes after night,
and spring after winter.

Rachel Carson

A Song of Joy from Osho

Look at the trees,
look at the birds,
look at the clouds,
look at the stars . . .
and if you have eyes
you will be able to see
that the whole existence is joyful.
Everything is simply happy.
Trees are happy for no reason;
they are not going to become prime ministers
or presidents
and they are not going to become rich
and they will never have any bank balance.
Look at the flowers — for no reason.
It is simply unbelievable
how happy flowers are.

*Consider how the wild flowers grow.
They do not labor or spin.
Yet I tell you, not even Solomon in all his splendor
was dressed like one of these.
If that is how God clothes the grass of the field,
which is here today,
and tomorrow is thrown into the fire,
how much more will he clothe you—
you of little faith!*

Jesus (Luke 12:28 NIV)

Psalm 104

Yahweh, my God, you are very great.
You are clothed with honor and majesty.
He covers himself with light as with a garment.
He stretches out the heavens like a curtain.
He lays the beams of his rooms in the waters.
He makes the clouds his chariot.
He walks on the wings of the wind.
He appointed the moon for seasons.
The sun knows when to set.
You make darkness, and it is night.
Yahweh, how many are your works!
In wisdom have you made them all.
The earth is full of your riches.
Bless Yahweh, my soul. Praise Yah!

5
Worshipping God in Nature

Every creature, which is in heaven, and on the earth, and under the earth, and such as are in the sea, and all that are in them: I heard all saying: To him that sitteth on the throne, and to the Lamb, benediction, and honour, and glory, and power, for ever and ever.

Revelation 5:13 DRB

We may think of worship as singing songs of praise or moments of loving prayer. The oldest version of the word "worship," however, meant literally "worth-ship"—the act of proclaiming and affirming another's worth, whether through song, word, action, or thought. The world of Nature is one of our many gateways into God's worth.

Deepening your understanding of the natural world can be a form a worship. If Nature is the revelation of God's very being, it should not only be celebrated but studied, for to know Nature is to know God. Gaze at the stars, attend lectures at a local university or nature center, watch wildlife and cosmology shows; learn about the tiny organisms that live in your body, or about weather patterns in your part of the world, or about the Big Bang and origins of the universe. This too is worship. Science and faith are not enemies; instead, a love for science can nourish your soul and glorify the Creator. The plants in your yard, the microbes in your body, and the stars in the sky are all expressions of the Divine nature. We live in a world where God reveals the miracle of grace in sky and leaf and stone. Even the tiny droplets of water in a rainbow color the world with their message of God's faithfulness.

Ultimately, we worship God best by loving God—and by loving the God-created world. Russian novelist Fydor Dostoevsky wrote, "Love all of God's creation, the whole of it and every grain of sand. Love every leaf, every ray of God's light! Love the animals, love the plants, and love everything. If you love everything, you will soon perceive the divine mystery in things. Once you perceive it, you will begin to comprehend it better every day. And you will come at last to love the whole world with an all-embracing love."

The Earth is an amazing place! Enjoy it. Love it. Pour out your heart to God in awe and wonder as you gaze at it. Worship the One who made Creation and who continues to live at the heart of Creation.

Psalm 148

Praise Yah!
Praise him, sun and moon!
Praise him, all you shining stars!
Praise him, you heavens of heavens,
You waters that are above the heavens.
Let them praise Yahweh's name,
for he commanded, and they were created.
He has also established them forever and ever.
He has made a decree which will not pass away.

Praise Yahweh from the earth,
you great sea creatures, and all depths;
lightning and hail, snow and clouds;
stormy wind, fulfilling his word;
mountains and all hills;
fruit trees and all cedars;
wild animals and all livestock;
small creatures and flying birds;
kings of the earth and all peoples;
princes and all judges of the earth;
both young men and maidens;
old men and children:
let them praise Yahweh's name,
for his name alone is exalted.

She could now think of the Father of Spirits . . .
as the root of every delight in the world,
at the heart of the horse she rode,
in the wind that blew joy into her. . . .
No wonder that with this well of living water in her heart
she should be glad—merry even, and ready for anything.

George MacDonald, from his novel *Donal Grant*

The Loves of Taliesin

Beautiful it is that God shall save me.
Beautiful too the bright fish in the lake,
Beautiful too the sun in the sky,
The beauty of an eagle on the shore
when the tide is full. . . .
Beautiful the covenant of the Creator with Earth,
The beauty in the wilderness of doe and fawn,
The beauty of wild leeks and the berries of harvest,
The beauty of the heather when it turns purple,
Beautiful the pastureland. . . .
The beauty of water shimmering,
The beauty of the world where the Trinity speaks,
But the loveliest of all is the Christ
Who lives in all beauty.

THE WHITE-WAVED SEA

I beseech Heaven and Earth,
I beseech the Earth's waters to help me.
May I not be abandoned,
may I find strength.
I adore the Lord
when I see the wondrous structures
of both Heaven and Earth:
bright heaven with angels,
green Earth with white-waved ocean.
Let us adore the Lord,
Maker of bright heaven with its angels,
and on Earth the white-waved sea.

Canticle of the Sun

Be praised, my Lord, through all Your creatures,
especially through my lord Brother Sun,
who brings the day; and You give light through him.
Of you, Most High, he bears the likeness.
Be praised, my Lord, through Sister Moon and the stars;
in the heavens You have made them,
precious and beautiful.
Be praised, my Lord, through Brothers Wind and Air
and clouds and storms, and all the weather,
through which You give Your creatures sustenance.
Be praised, My Lord, through Sister Water;
she is very useful, and humble, and precious, and pure.

Be praised, my Lord, through Brother Fire,
through whom You brighten the night.
He is beautiful and cheerful, and powerful and strong.
Be praised, my Lord, through our sister Mother Earth,
who feeds us and rules us.

Holy Mass Among the Trees

I was in a pleasant place today
beneath mantles of green hazel
listening at break of day
to the bright thrush
singing a splendid verse
of fluent phrases deep with meaning.
Fleet of wing, sweet-throated,
he was love's brown go-between
carrying messages from Heaven.

More skilled than any priest,
his vestments were brown wings,
his green mantle was the wind.
The altar's canopy was gold-bright leaves,
and the chanting of the gospel
was bright and long,
faultless and unfaultering.
Upon every tree, each leaf was like a wafer.
The lark sang out the holy bell.
The scarlet bush raised high the sacrifice
in adoration to the Holy One.
I drank deep from the cup,
amid the gentle grove of birch.

The Glory of God in Nature

The sun when he appears,
bringing tidings as he goes forth,
Is a marvelous instrument,
the work of the Most High:
At his noon he dries up the country,
And who shall stand against his burning heat?

Great is the Lord that made him;
And at his word he hastens his course.
The moon also is in all things for her season,
For a declaration of times, and a sign of the world.
From the moon is the sign of the feast day;
A light that wanes when she is come to the full.

The month is called after her name,
Increasing wonderfully in her changing;
An instrument of the army on high,
Shining forth in the firmament of heaven;

Look upon the rainbow, and praise him that made it;
Exceeding beautiful in the brightness thereof.
It encircles the heaven round about with a circle of glory;
The hands of the Most High have stretched it.

***Heaven is under our feet
as well as over our heads.***

Henry David Thoreau

When Morning Gilds the Skies

When morning gilds the skies, my heart awaking cries:
May Jesus Christ be praised!
Alike at work and prayer, to Jesus I repair:
May Jesus Christ be praised!
When you begin the day, O never fail to say,
May Jesus Christ be praised!

Let earth's wide circle round
in joyful notes resound:
May Jesus Christ be praised!

Let air and sea and sky
from depth to height reply:
May Jesus Christ be praised!

And at your work rejoice, to sing with heart and voice,
May Jesus Christ be praised!
Sing, suns and stars of space, sing, ye that see His face,
Sing, Jesus Christ be praised!
God's whole creation o'er, for aye and evermore
Shall Jesus Christ be praised!

Some keep the Sabbath going to Church,
I keep it staying at Home—
With a bobolink for a Chorister,
And an Orchard, for a Dome.

Emily Dickinson

AT IMBOLC

Imbolc is February first and the beginning of Celtic spring. It is associated with Saint Brigid, and the coming of spring is symbolically understood as Brigid spreading her colorful mantle over the barren earth.

I thank you, Lord, for the wisdom of the ancestors,
who marked the coming of spring in bleak February.
For shining-bright Brigid!
For Candlemas Day,
when tradition tells us to be sure to have
half our wood and half our hay.
For the groundhog lumbering out of his den.
For the lengthening day and the higher-arcing sun.
For the drip of icicle at the eave.

For the spring that starts on a snowy day.
For a spring eternal
in the Word of your beloved Child.

On this day, your Son the Light of the World
was presented in the temple:
Let me rejoice in the coming of light!
On this day sweet Brigid's eternal flames
bring new light to the earth:
May I rejoice at the coming of light!
All praise and all thanksgiving
to the God of the Springtime,
As the icicle drips
and the dawn comes ever-earlier!

Thanks to Thee

Thanks to Thee, O God,
that I have risen today.
Thanks to Thee, O God of every gift,
for the rising of this life itself
in sun and sap, in field and fell.
I praise Thee, O great God,
that as you clothe my body in wool,
Thou dost also clothe the Earth with cloud,
with summer warmth and autumn chill,
to Thine own glory, O God,
and to the glory of the Earth,
and to my soul likewise.

And as the sun scatters the mist
on the crest of the hills,
may all haze clear from my soul, O God.
May I see Thee true in the wheeling sky
and praise Thee evermore,
O great God of every gift.

Ruler of the Galaxies

I set my sights on the heavens,
my eyes sharp as an eagle's,
and gaze as far as I can
into the starry sky.

Creator, be in my eyes.
Child of God, expand my vision.
Spirit, fill me with starlight.

Behold the Milky Way,
that vast spiral galaxy,
Earth's home
(our world but a spot on the rim).

Creator, the world is too wondrous!
Child of God, such a marvel I see wherever I turn.
Spirit, expand my heart to take it in.

I gaze in awe at suns uncountable:
red giants, blue giants,
supernovas, pulsars and dwarfs,
hydrogen fires a million times the brightness
of our own little sun.

Creator, what fires You've kindled!
Child, what have You birthed?
Spirit, I might explode like a supernova
with joy.

No doubt innumerable other worlds
shine in space,
filled with gasses and waters and lands,
plants and creatures
I cannot even imagine.

Creator made all this.
Christ loves all this.
Spirit dwells in every particle.
Glory to the All-Maker!
Glory to the Child!
Glory to the Breath of Life!

Be praised in the wheeling gas clouds.
Be praised in the flashing meteor.
Be praised in the star nursery where light is born.
God of the immeasurable universe,
You are everywhere present in space,
and You live inside of me.

Let me never doubt Your power
Let me never doubt Your love.
Let me never doubt Your wisdom.

Star Maker, rule my heart.

GLORIOUS LORD

Hail to you, glorious Lord!
May church and chancel praise you.
May plain and hillside praise you.
May the the springs and rivers praise you.
May darkness and light praise you,
and the cedar and the sweet fruit tree.
May life everlasting praise you.
May the birds and the bees praise you.
May the re-growth of green and the grass praise you.
May male and female praise you.
May books and letters praise you.
May thought and action praise you.
And I too shall praise you, Lord of glory!

The Isle of Arran

This ancient Celtic poem may not strictly be a prayer, but the poet's soul is obviously filled with appreciation for the beauty of the island. When the soul pours out joy, is that not a prayer of worship?

Arran of the many stags,
the sea strikes against its shoulder,
isle in which companies are fed,
ridge on which blue spears are reddened.
skittish deer are on her peaks,
delicious berries on her manes,
cool water in her rivers,
mast upon her dun oaks.

Greyhounds are in it and beagles,
blackberries and sloes of the dark blackthorn,
her dwellings close against the woods,
deer scattered about her oak-woods,
gleaning of purple upon her rocks,
faultless grass upon her slopes,
over her fair shapely crags
noise of dappled fawns a-skipping.
Smooth is her level land,
fat are her swine,
bright are her fields,
her nuts upon the tops of her hazel-wood,
long galleys sailing past her.
Delightful it is when the fair season comes,
trout under the brinks of her rivers,
seagulls answer each other round her white cliff,
delightful at all times is Arran!

The Prayer of the Three in the Fire

O you heavens, bless you the Lord:
praise and exalt him above all forever.
O you sun and moon, bless you the Lord:
praise and exalt him above all forever.
O you stars of heaven, bless you the Lord:
praise and exalt him above all forever.
O every shower and dew, bless you the Lord:
praise and exalt him above all forever
O all you winds, bless you the Lord:
praise and exalt him above all forever.
O you fire and heat, bless you the Lord:
praise and exalt him above all forever.

O you nights and days, bless you the Lord:
praise and exalt him above all forever.
O you light and darkness, bless you the Lord:
praise and exalt him above all forever.
O you cold and heat, bless you the Lord:
praise and exalt him above all forever.
O you frost and snow, bless you the Lord:
praise and exalt him above all forever.
O you lightnings and clouds, bless you the Lord:
praise and exalt him above all forever.
O let the earth bless the Lord:
let it praise and exalt him above all forever.

O you mountains and hills, bless you the Lord:
>   praise and exalt him above all forever.
> O all you things that grow on the earth,
>   bless you the Lord:
>   praise and exalt him above all forever.
> O sea and rivers, bless you the Lord:
>   praise and exalt him above all forever.
> O you springs, bless you the Lord:
>   praise and exalt him above all forever.
> O you whales, and all that move in the waters,
>   bless you the Lord:
>   praise and exalt him above all forever.

O all you fowls of the air, bless you the Lord:
praise and exalt him above all forever.
O all you beasts and cattle, bless you the Lord:
praise and exalt him above all forever.
O you children of men, bless you the Lord:
praise and exalt him above all forever.

Psalm 19

The heavens declare the glory of God.
The expanse shows his handiwork.
Day after day they pour out speech,
and night after night they display knowledge.
There is no speech nor language,
where their voice is not heard.
Their voice has gone out through all the earth,
their words to the end of the world.
In them he has set a tent for the sun,
which is as a bridegroom coming out of his room,
like a strong man rejoicing to run his course.
His going out is from the end of the heavens,
his circuit to its ends;
There is nothing hidden from its heat.

Thanksgiving for the Earth

O God, we thank You for this earth, our home;
for the wide sky and the blessed sun,
for the salt sea and the running water,
for the everlasting hills and the never-resting winds,
for trees and the common grass underfoot.
We thank You for our senses
by which we hear the songs of birds,
and see the splendor of the summer fields,
and taste of the autumn fruits,
and rejoice in the feel of the snow,
and smell the breath of spring.

Grant us a heart wide open to all this beauty;
and save our souls from being so blind
that we pass unseeing
when even the common thorn-bush
is aflame with your glory, O God our creator,
who lives and reigns forever and ever.

Sources

Page 16: "Prayer Rock," Kenneth McIntosh.

Page 18: "God in All Things," *Carmina Gadelica*, a compendium of prayers, hymns, charms, and blessings that folklorist Alexander Carmichael gathered and recorded between 1860 and 1909 from ordinary people living in Scotland.

Page 20: "The Song of Amergin," translated from the *Book of Leinster*, a twelfth-century compilation of even more ancient Gaelic literature and mythology.

Page 22: "A Simple Touch," Marsha McIntosh.

Page 23: "The Likeness of the Lord," *Carmina Gadelica*.

Page 24: "King of All Nature," *Carmina Gadelica*.

Page 25: "God of the Moon, God of the Sun," Carmina Gadelica.

Page 26: "The Hermit's Song," attributed to Saint Manchán mac Silláin who died in 664; translated from Gaelic by Gerard Murphy in *Early Irish Lyrics* (Clarendon Press, 1956).

Page 27: "Prayer of the Green Place," Ellyn Sanna.

Page 29: "The Healing of Empty Places," Kenneth McIntosh.

Page 30: "God's Presence," Ellyn Sanna.

Page 33: "Night," Marsha McIntosh.

Page 34: "Prayer of the New Moon," *Carmina Gadelica*.

Page 35: "Morning," Marsha McIntosh.

SOURCES

Page 37: "Look No Farther," Ellyn Sanna.

Page 39: "God's Song," Ellyn Sanna.

Page 42: "God's Hand Held Out," Ellyn Sanna, inspired by the ancient Irish benediction that's included here on page 74.

Page 44: "Christ in Creatures," Ellyn Sanna, inspired in part by an ancient Celtic rune of hospitality.

Page 47: "Open My Ears," Ellyn Sanna.

Page 48: "Open My Eyes," Ellyn Sanna.

Page 50: "God Is Speaking," Ellyn Sanna.

Page 52: "Hymn to the Presence of God," Ellyn Sanna.

Page 58: "The Earth's Blessings," adapted from a traditional Irish benediction.

Page 61: "Prayer of Blessing," adapted from the *Carmina Gadelica*. Celtic prayers were often repetitive, wrapping blessing upon blessing around a person until she was surrounded in benediction.

Page 64: "A Child's Blessing," Ellyn Sanna.

Page 67: "Cradle Song," Ellyn Sanna, adapted from a traditional Irish lullaby. Isaac Watts, the eighteenth-century hymnwriter, wrote another adaptation of this ancient song.

Page 70: "A Prayer for a Friend," Ellyn Sanna, inspired by a traditional Irish benediction.

Page 73: " Clouds," Marsha McIntosh.

Page 74: "Irish Benediction," an ancient travelers' blessing.

Page 75: "The Earth's Deep Peace," William Sharp. Sharp was a nineteenth-century Scottish

SOURCES

author, who also wrote under the name Fiona MacLeod. He included this prayer in several of his works, including a translated collection of ancient traditional Gaelic poems and prayers.

Page 78: "Thanksgiving," adapted from a traditional prayer from the Haudenosaunee people. Native American peoples' perspective on Nature was very similar to the ancient Celts'; both cultures saw no separation between the natural world and the spiritual world. Both saw Divine revelation and love in Nature's beauty and bounty.

Page 80: "Come I This Day," adapted from the *Carmina Gadelica*.

Page 82: "I Have No Need of a Kingdom," attributed to Saint Marbhan. Marbhan was a sixth-century Irish saint whose brother was Guaire, King of Connacht. This poem is said to be Marbhan's response to his brother when the king asked him to return to his comfortable home.

Page 84: "A Small Place in the Wilderness," included in *Ancient Irish Poetry* by Kuno Meyer (1911).

Page 89: "Blessings Everywhere," Kenneth McIntosh.

Page 91: "Saint Patrick's Breastplate." Loricas (breastplates) were ancient Celtic prayers of protection. The Lorica of Saint Patrick is a very ancient and oft-repeated prayer for protection against all manner of evil. In this portion, the saint calls the forces of nature to his aid.

Page 92: "Rain," Marsha McIntosh.

Page 93: "A Chant for Columba's Plant," *Carmina Gadelica*.

Page 98: "Lady Earth," adapted from the *Carmina Gadelica*.

Page 100: "Great Spirit Prayer," Big Thunder (Bedagi), a late nineteenth-century Algonquin.

Sources

Page 101: "The Shield of God," Ellyn Sanna.

Page 104: "Beltane Blessing," *Carmina Gadelica*.

Page 106: "Blessing for the Reaping," *Carmina Gadelica*.

Page 107: "A Prayer of Protection for the Earth," Kenneth McIntosh.

Page 108: "St. Basil's Prayer of Compassion." Saint Basil was a fourth-century Greek bishop.

Page 109: "Prayer for a Wounded Earth," Ellyn Sanna.

Page 111: "Prayer for the Earth During Climate Change," Ellyn Sanna.

Page 116: "Messages from God," Ellyn Sanna.

Page 119: "The Seasons," Ellyn Sanna.

Page 121: "Heaven and Earth Are One," Ellyn Sanna.

Page 123: "Today's Work," Ellyn Sanna.

Page 125: "Ebb and Flow," Ellyn Sanna.

Page 127: "Fly Free," adapted from a traditional Irish prayer.

Page 129: "Prayer at a Loved One's Death," Ellyn Sanna.

Page 132: "The Archangels' Blessing of the Days," adapted from the *Carmina Gadelica*.

Page 136: "Earth, Teach Me," a Ute prayer.

Page 138: "A Song of Joy from Osho." Osho was a twentieth-century Indian mystic and spiritual teacher.

Page 140: Psalm 104:1–3, 19, 20, 24, 35, World English Bible.

Sources

Page 144: Psalm 148: 1, 3–13, World English Bible.

Page 147: "The Loves of Taliesin," attributed to the legendary fifth-century Welsh bard.

Page 149: "Canticle of the Sun," by Saint Francis of Assisi. Francis lived in Italy centuries after the golden age of Celtic Christianity, but he was one of the Celts' spiritual children, since the legacy of Irish traveler Columbanus (who founded a monastery in Italy) influenced Francis to seek God's presence in Nature.

Page 151: "Holy Mass Among the Trees," Dafydd ap Gwilym, fourteenth-century Welsh poet.

Page 153: "The Glory of God in Nature," Sirach 43. The Book of Sirach is part of what is sometimes referred to the Apocrypha; it would have been standard in all the Bibles copied and handed down by Celtic scribes.

Page 156: "When Morning Gilds the Skies," eighteenth-century German hymn, translated by Joseph Barnby (1868).

Page 159: "At Imbolc," William Palmer.

Page 161: "Thanks to Thee," adapted from the *Carmina Gadelica*.

Page 163: "Ruler of the Galaxies," Kenneth McIntosh.

Page 168: "Glorious Lord," tenth-century Welsh. This prayer is a good example of Celtic spirituality at its best, sweeping up into its embrace all of life with a grand and jubilant inclusiveness.

Page 169: "The Isle of Arran," from a thirteenth-century Irish poem.

SOURCES

Page 170: "The Prayer of the Three in the Fire,"
Daniel 3:36–60, James Platter translation (2012). Shadrach, Meshach, and Abednego, three Hebrew young men, were condemned to death in a fiery furnace by Nebuchadnezzar, king of Babylon, because they refused to worship any god but the God of Israel. The king sees four men walking in the flames, the fourth "like a son of god."

Page 174: Psalm 19:1–6, World English Bible.

Page 175: "Thanksgiving for the Earth," Walter Rauschenbusch (1861–1918).

Water from an Ancient Well: Celtic Spirituality for Modern Life
Pilgrimage Study Edition

Kenneth McIntosh

This new version has more than 150 pages of previously unpublished material, including illustrated guides to Celtic pilgrimage sites, study questions, and updated research.

Using story, scripture, reflection, and prayer, Kenneth McIntosh offers us a taste of the living water that refreshed the ancient Celts, allowing them to perceive God as a living Presence in everybody and everything. This Earth-based and inclusive perspective suggests life-giving alternatives to modern faith practices, opening the door to a Christianity big enough to embrace the entire world.

"If you want to run away to paradise for a couple of days, and drink living water from a source unlike any other, read Kenneth McIntosh's deeply satisfying book."
— Leonard Sweet, best-selling author of *Nudge: Awakening Each Other to the God Who's Already There* and *So Beautiful: Divine Design for Life and the Church*

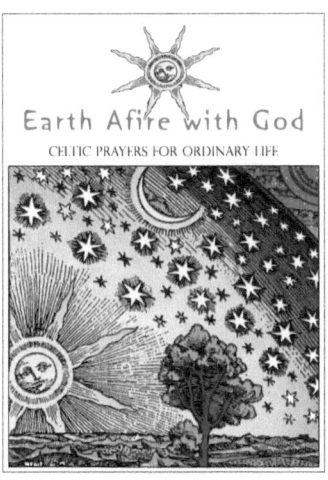

Earth Afire with God: Celtic Prayers for Ordinary Life

Anamchara Books

Here are prayers and blessings to sanctify your daily life. They will remind you to look for the holiness of the everyday; they will show you the real presence of God in Creation. Illumine your life with the ancient Celts' perspective on prayer. Each glimpse we have of the Earth's beauty, each ordinary sound we hear, every bite of food we eat, and even our daily routines, can all reveal God.

Kenneth McIntosh, author of *Water from an Ancient Well, Celtic Spirituality for Modern Life*, writes, "This book knocks the dust off ancient treasures—such as selections from the Carmina Gadelica—and also introduces some lovely new prayers, all written from the Celtic perspective."

The Thread

Lucie Stone

Fifteen-year-old Callie follows a mysterious thread that pulls her through the night, deep into the terrible secrets of her own life. Meanwhile, Kirin hears his dead brother calling him, leading him to revelations that will change his entire world. Together, Callie and Kirin navigate a dark tide of old, long-buried evil that sweeps them both from their familiar reality and into a world they never suspected existed.

"If Madeleine L'Engle had collaborated with the authors of *The Lovely Bones* and *The Life of Pi*, the result might have looked a lot like this. Stone tackles the darkness of sexual abuse and murder, while offering a multi-faith roadmap to hope and healing."
—Kenneth McIntosh, M. Div., author of *Water from an Ancient Well: Celtic Spirituality for Modern Life* and *Magic Reversed*

Magic Reversed

Kenneth McIntosh

Like *The Thread*, this book can be enjoyed on several levels. It's an action-packed young adult fantasy, brimming with adventure, danger, and romance. Young adult readers will relate to the tension between Finn and Freya that slowly blossoms into something deeper. Fantasy-lovers of all ages will be delighted to encounter characters from Celtic mythology: the wizard Merlin, the Goddess Brigid, and the ravenous walking dead spawned by the Dark Lord's cauldron. At the same time, those who are attracted to Celtic spirituality will find strands of symbolism, like gold threads in an ancient tapestry, meshed unobtrusively with this tale of a young hero's journey to save his world.

Anamchara Books
Books to Inspire Your Spiritual Journey

In Celtic Christianity, an *anamchara* is a soul friend, a companion and mentor (often across the miles and the years) on the spiritual journey. Soul friendship entails a commitment to both accept and challenge, to reach across all divisions in a search for the wisdom and truth at the heart of our lives.

At Anamchara Books, we are committed to creating a community of soul friends by publishing books that lead us into deeper relationships with God, the Earth, and each other. These books connect us with the great mystics of the past, as well as with more modern spiritual thinkers. They are designed to build bridges, shaping an inclusive spirituality where we all can grow.

To find out more about Anamchara Books and order our books, visit www.AnamcharaBooks.com today.

Anamchara Books
www.AnamcharaBooks.com

www.ingramcontent.com/pod-product-compliance
Lightning Source LLC
Chambersburg PA
CBHW060524080526
44586CB00012B/598